THE NVIDIA-SALESFORCE PARTNERSHIP
Future of AI and Human Collaboration

How Autonomous Artificial Intelligence Will Redefine Industries

J. Andy Peters

Copyright ©**J. Andy Peters, *2024*.**

All rights reserved. No part of this publication may be reproduced, distributed, or transmitted in any form or by any means, including photocopying, recording, or other electronic or mechanical methods, without the prior written permission of the publisher, except in the case of brief quotations embodied in critical reviews and certain other noncommercial uses permitted by copyright law.

Table of Contents

Introduction..3
Chapter 1: The Rise of AI in Business........................6
Chapter 2: Deep Dive into the Salesforce and NVIDIA Partnership..11
Chapter 3: The Role of Autonomous AI Agents...... 16
Chapter 4: Transforming Industries..........................21
Chapter 5: The Human-AI Collaboration.................. 30
Chapter 6: The Future of AI: What's Next?.............. 36
Conclusion.. 41

Introduction

The world is witnessing one of the most transformative periods in history: the **AI revolution**. In just a few short decades, artificial intelligence has shifted from being a futuristic concept to an integral part of everyday life. From self-driving cars to smart assistants, AI is increasingly influencing how we work, live, and interact with technology. What was once the realm of science fiction is now a driving force in industries across the globe. But this revolution is far from complete. We are on the cusp of a new era, one where **autonomous AI systems** will not only augment human capabilities but could eventually operate independently across various sectors—reshaping industries and creating entirely new markets in the process.

At the forefront of this revolution are two tech giants: **Salesforce** and **NVIDIA**. Their groundbreaking partnership represents a bold step forward in the evolution of AI, combining the strengths of **Salesforce's cloud-based customer relationship management (CRM) and NVIDIA's cutting-edge graphics processing units (GPUs)**. Together, they are unlocking new potential in AI technology, enabling more powerful, efficient, and intelligent systems that can handle complex tasks with ease. This partnership has the potential to disrupt the way businesses operate, enhance customer experiences, and redefine the future of AI-human collaboration.

The objective of this book is to provide a comprehensive analysis of this transformative partnership and its far-reaching implications. Through detailed reporting, storytelling, and expert analysis, this book will explore:

1. **The role of AI in shaping the future**: We'll dive into the ongoing AI revolution, its impact on various industries, and the promise of autonomous AI agents.
2. **The Salesforce-NVIDIA collaboration**: An in-depth look at the technological synergies

between Salesforce's cloud infrastructure and NVIDIA's AI capabilities, and how their combined efforts are pushing the boundaries of what AI can do.

3. **How businesses can adapt and thrive**: We'll explore how organizations can leverage AI to stay ahead in an increasingly competitive marketplace, and the role this partnership will play in shaping the future of enterprise solutions.

4. **Key challenges and opportunities**: We'll discuss the ethical, social, and technological challenges that come with the rise of autonomous AI systems and how businesses and individuals can navigate these complexities.

By the end of this book, readers will have a clear understanding of the **Salesforce-NVIDIA partnership** and its potential to transform industries across the board, as well as insights into the evolving role of AI in our everyday lives.

Chapter 1: The Rise of AI in Business

Artificial Intelligence is no longer a concept of the future; it is a driving force reshaping industries across the globe. From healthcare to finance, from manufacturing to marketing, AI is fundamentally changing how businesses operate, how products are made, and how services are delivered. Companies are harnessing AI to improve efficiency, innovate at an unprecedented pace, and solve complex problems that were once thought unsolvable.

The ability of AI to analyze vast amounts of data, recognize patterns, and make predictions has already transformed business decision-making. In industries like healthcare, AI-powered tools are being used for early disease detection, personalized treatments, and even robotic surgeries. In finance, algorithms now analyze market trends and execute trades in milliseconds. AI is making operations faster, smarter, and more personalized, providing both opportunities and challenges for businesses to navigate.

But as AI continues to evolve, its impact deepens. New applications of AI are being explored daily, with the potential to disrupt even the most established industries. This is why the partnership between Salesforce and NVIDIA is so crucial. As two giants in their respective fields, their collaboration promises to accelerate AI development and integrate these powerful technologies into even more sectors, leading to a new era of AI-driven innovation.

At present, AI is rapidly advancing through multiple domains. From natural language processing (NLP) that powers chatbots and virtual assistants, to computer vision that enables machines to "see" and understand the world, AI technologies are reaching new heights. Machine learning (ML) algorithms are improving at an exponential rate, enabling AI systems to adapt and optimize in real-time. Deep learning, a subset of ML, is allowing machines to perform tasks once considered exclusive to human intelligence, such as understanding context, generating creative work, and even composing music.

Yet, despite these advancements, we are still in the early stages of what AI can truly achieve. AI remains limited in many ways. Current systems are often siloed, requiring specialized knowledge and vast amounts of data to operate effectively. Additionally, ethical concerns about privacy, bias, and transparency continue to challenge the industry, requiring careful attention as technologies evolve.

As we stand on the cusp of AI's next major leap, the partnership between Salesforce and NVIDIA is poised to accelerate progress. By combining Salesforce's robust customer relationship management (CRM) platform with NVIDIA's powerful computing technologies, the partnership promises to bring AI to new frontiers. The development of autonomous AI agents, capable of performing tasks with minimal human input, is one of the key innovations that could redefine entire industries in the coming years.

As the AI revolution unfolds, two industry giants are at the forefront of reshaping how artificial intelligence integrates into everyday business operations: **Salesforce** and **NVIDIA**. Their strategic partnership marks a new era in AI-driven innovation, bringing together the power of cloud computing, AI models, and real-time data analysis to create groundbreaking solutions for businesses across various sectors.

Salesforce, known for its pioneering Customer Relationship Management (CRM) platform, has long been a leader in leveraging technology to streamline business operations and improve customer engagement. With AI integration, Salesforce aims to further enhance its capabilities, automating tasks, offering predictive insights, and delivering personalized experiences at an unprecedented scale.

NVIDIA, a leader in graphics processing units (GPUs) and artificial intelligence hardware, brings unmatched computing power to the table. Their innovations in AI hardware and software have made it possible for businesses to run complex AI models, accelerating the deployment of intelligent systems that can learn, adapt, and make decisions on their own.

Together, Salesforce and NVIDIA are not just pushing the boundaries of AI—they're defining them. By merging Salesforce's CRM expertise with NVIDIA's cutting-edge AI technologies, they are creating new opportunities for businesses to optimize operations, foster innovation, and enhance customer experiences in ways never before possible.

Chapter 2: Deep Dive into the Salesforce and NVIDIA Partnership

To understand the significance of the partnership between Salesforce and NVIDIA, it's important to first explore the remarkable histories of these two companies, each of which has played a pivotal role in shaping the future of technology.

Salesforce, founded in 1999 by Marc Benioff, started with a bold vision: to revolutionize the way businesses manage customer relationships. The company's pioneering efforts in cloud computing transformed the enterprise software industry, moving traditional customer relationship management (CRM) systems to the cloud. Today, Salesforce is a global leader, providing a suite of products that leverage AI, machine learning, and data analytics to help organizations optimize customer engagement and drive business growth.

On the other hand, **NVIDIA**, founded in 1993 by Jensen Huang, Chris Malachowsky, and Curtis

Priem, began with a focus on high-performance graphics processing units (GPUs) for gaming. However, NVIDIA quickly pivoted into more complex computing solutions, becoming a major player in AI and deep learning technologies. The company's GPUs have become the backbone of AI research and innovation, powering everything from autonomous vehicles to cloud-based AI models. Today, NVIDIA is a key player in the development of AI infrastructure, providing the hardware and software needed to accelerate the next generation of intelligent machines.

Together, Salesforce and NVIDIA represent the convergence of cloud-based customer relationship management and high-performance AI computing. Their partnership not only underscores their shared vision for the future of AI but also sets the stage for breakthroughs that will redefine industries across the globe.

The partnership between Salesforce and NVIDIA is a bold step into the future, fueled by a shared vision to revolutionize how artificial intelligence is integrated into business processes. Both companies have long been at the forefront of technological innovation—Salesforce as a leader in customer relationship management (CRM) and cloud-based solutions, and NVIDIA as a pioneer in graphics processing units (GPUs) and AI infrastructure. By joining forces, they aim to unlock the full potential of AI to transform industries across the globe.

At the heart of this collaboration is the goal to empower businesses to harness the power of autonomous AI agents. These agents will be capable of performing tasks traditionally handled by humans, but at a speed and scale never before possible. Salesforce brings its expertise in customer data and business automation, while NVIDIA contributes its cutting-edge AI hardware and software, enabling companies to process vast amounts of data and generate insights in real time.

Their shared vision is to create AI-driven ecosystems where businesses can operate more efficiently, deliver hyper-personalized customer experiences, and make data-driven decisions faster than ever. The collaboration between Salesforce and NVIDIA aims to drive the next wave of innovation, bridging the gap between traditional business operations and the AI-powered future.

The technological advancements emerging from the Salesforce-NVIDIA partnership are nothing short of groundbreaking. At the core of this collaboration lies the integration of NVIDIA's powerful GPUs with Salesforce's robust suite of cloud applications. This fusion enables the creation of AI models that are not only faster but more capable of handling complex tasks.

One of the primary breakthroughs is the development of **autonomous AI agents**. These agents are designed to interact with customers, understand their needs, and provide instant solutions—without human intervention. Powered by NVIDIA's GPUs, these agents can analyze large datasets, learn from past interactions, and predict future customer behaviors, all in real-time. For businesses, this translates into enhanced operational efficiency and the ability to offer personalized services at scale.

Additionally, the integration of NVIDIA's **AI supercomputing capabilities** into Salesforce's platform allows for deeper insights and predictive analytics. Businesses can now leverage AI models that were previously too resource-intensive to run on traditional systems. With the ability to process data faster and more accurately, companies can make strategic decisions with a level of confidence that was previously unattainable.

Beyond autonomous agents, the partnership has accelerated advancements in **natural language processing (NLP),** enabling more intuitive human-AI interactions. Customers can now communicate with AI systems in a more conversational manner, while businesses can gain richer insights from customer feedback, reviews, and social media conversations.

Chapter 3: The Role of Autonomous AI Agents

Autonomous AI agents represent a groundbreaking evolution in artificial intelligence technology. Unlike traditional AI systems, which require constant input and supervision from human operators, autonomous AI agents are designed to function independently, making decisions, performing tasks, and adapting to new environments with minimal human intervention.

These agents are powered by advanced machine learning algorithms, neural networks, and natural language processing systems that enable them to analyze complex data, identify patterns, and optimize actions in real time. Essentially, autonomous AI agents are capable of learning from experience, improving their performance over time, and operating without the need for constant human guidance.

In the context of the Salesforce and NVIDIA partnership, autonomous AI agents are poised to redefine the way industries function. From customer service automation to predictive analytics, these agents will transform workflows, reduce operational costs, and improve efficiency by taking over tasks that were previously handled by humans. What makes them truly revolutionary is their ability to think, reason, and even adapt their decision-making processes as they process more data.

For companies like Salesforce, which has long been a leader in customer relationship management (CRM), autonomous AI agents will drive innovation by enabling more personalized, responsive, and scalable customer experiences. NVIDIA, known for its powerful graphics processing units (GPUs), provides the computational power needed to support the massive datasets and complex algorithms that autonomous agents require to function effectively.

The combination of these two technological giants, each bringing unique strengths to the table, sets the stage for a new era in AI development—one where machines no longer simply follow instructions but actively learn and evolve to meet the needs of their environments.

The rise of autonomous AI agents holds the potential to revolutionize how businesses operate at every level. These AI-driven systems are designed to function independently, capable of making decisions, optimizing workflows, and delivering insights without the need for continuous human intervention. In practice, they can automate complex processes, predict customer behaviors, and even perform tasks traditionally requiring human intelligence. For businesses, this means increased efficiency, reduced operational costs, and the ability to scale operations faster than ever before.

For instance, in customer service, AI agents can handle routine inquiries, analyze customer sentiment, and resolve issues in real-time, all while learning from each interaction to improve their responses over time. In industries like finance, healthcare, and logistics, autonomous AI agents are already being used to optimize supply chains, predict market trends, and assist in decision-making processes.

While the potential of fully autonomous AI systems is vast, their integration into business operations is not without challenges. One of the primary concerns is the balance between automation and human oversight. As businesses lean more on autonomous systems, ensuring that AI decisions align with company values, regulatory standards, and ethical considerations will be essential.

Another challenge is the risk of over-reliance on AI, where human judgment might be sidelined in favor of efficiency or cost savings. This raises the question of accountability—who is responsible when an AI system makes a critical error or fails to deliver on its predictions? In addition, there are concerns around data privacy, security, and bias in AI decision-making.

However, despite these hurdles, the potential benefits of autonomous systems far outweigh the challenges. As AI technology continues to evolve, we can expect to see smarter, more efficient agents capable of handling a broader range of tasks with greater accuracy, further transforming business landscapes across industries.

Chapter 4: Transforming Industries

Autonomous AI agents are poised to have transformative effects across a variety of industries, revolutionizing the way businesses operate and interact with customers. Their potential to streamline operations, reduce costs, and improve decision-making is driving innovation in multiple sectors.

1. Healthcare

In healthcare, AI is already reshaping patient care and administrative processes. Autonomous AI agents can process vast amounts of medical data and provide real-time insights that help doctors make more accurate diagnoses. They can also assist with personalized treatment plans by analyzing patient history, genetic data, and other variables. For example, IBM's Watson Health uses AI to analyze data from clinical trials and electronic health records, offering decision support to healthcare professionals.

Moreover, AI-powered chatbots and virtual assistants are improving the patient experience by providing 24/7 support, answering queries, and scheduling appointments. Autonomous systems like these can reduce administrative burdens, allowing healthcare providers to focus more on patient care.

2. Finance

In the financial sector, autonomous AI agents are revolutionizing everything from fraud detection to personalized banking. AI systems can monitor transactions in real-time, identifying unusual activity that could indicate fraud. These systems use machine learning to adapt and improve their detection capabilities over time.

Additionally, AI is enhancing customer service in banking through intelligent virtual assistants that can handle inquiries, provide investment advice, and even help with complex financial planning. These systems enable financial institutions to offer highly personalized services while cutting costs and improving operational efficiency.

For example, JPMorgan Chase has implemented an AI-powered tool called COiN (Contract Intelligence) that analyzes legal documents and extracts valuable data, significantly speeding up the process of reviewing contracts and reducing human error.

3. Retail

The retail industry is embracing AI to enhance both customer experience and operational efficiency. AI-driven recommendation systems are increasingly common on e-commerce platforms, offering personalized product suggestions based on browsing history, preferences, and purchase patterns. This leads to higher sales conversions and customer satisfaction.

AI is also transforming supply chain management by predicting demand trends, optimizing inventory levels, and reducing waste. Autonomous robots are being used in warehouses for tasks such as sorting and packaging, speeding up logistics and reducing the need for human labor.

A notable example is Amazon's use of AI in its fulfillment centers, where robots work alongside humans to quickly retrieve products and prepare orders for shipment.

4. Manufacturing

In the manufacturing sector, autonomous AI agents are automating complex tasks, improving production efficiency, and enhancing quality control. AI-powered systems can predict when equipment will need maintenance, reducing downtime and extending the lifespan of machinery.

For instance, General Electric uses AI to predict failures in its gas turbines and jet engines, allowing for proactive maintenance that prevents costly breakdowns. AI also plays a role in optimizing production lines by adjusting processes in real time based on data from sensors, ensuring that manufacturing operations are as efficient as possible.

Examples of AI Applications in Business

1. Salesforce and NVIDIA's Partnership: Pioneering the Future of AI

One of the most notable examples of AI transforming business operations is the groundbreaking partnership between Salesforce and NVIDIA. By combining Salesforce's cloud-based customer relationship management (CRM) capabilities with NVIDIA's GPU-accelerated AI tools, the two companies are empowering businesses to leverage autonomous AI agents in ways previously unimaginable.

For example, Salesforce's Einstein AI platform can now utilize NVIDIA's powerful GPUs to process large datasets, providing businesses with deeper insights into customer behavior, predicting future trends, and automating routine tasks. This collaboration is setting the stage for a new era of AI-driven customer experiences.

2. AI in Healthcare: PathAI's Diagnostic Tools

In healthcare, PathAI is an AI company that uses deep learning algorithms to assist pathologists in diagnosing diseases like cancer from pathology images. Their AI-powered platform can analyze medical images with higher accuracy than human pathologists, leading to faster and more reliable diagnoses. PathAI's technology is already being used in hospitals around the world to improve patient outcomes and reduce diagnostic errors.

3. AI in Retail: Alibaba's Use of AI in Logistics

In retail, Alibaba has developed an AI-driven logistics system that optimizes the delivery process. The company uses machine learning algorithms to predict which products are likely to be in demand in specific locations, enabling them to pre-emptively ship inventory to the most strategic warehouses. This AI-powered system has helped Alibaba reduce delivery times and costs, improving customer satisfaction and increasing operational efficiency.

AI is fundamentally reshaping how businesses operate, making operations more efficient, enhancing decision-making, and providing exceptional customer experiences. With powerful algorithms and data-driven insights, AI helps companies to streamline processes, reduce costs, and offer personalized services at a scale that was once unimaginable.

Efficiency: AI automates repetitive tasks, allowing businesses to operate with greater speed and accuracy. For example, in customer support, AI-driven chatbots handle a large volume of routine inquiries, freeing human agents to focus on more complex issues. In supply chain management, AI optimizes logistics, predicting demand and adjusting inventories in real-time, which reduces waste and ensures products are delivered on time.

Decision-Making: One of the greatest strengths of AI is its ability to process vast amounts of data quickly and accurately. By analyzing historical trends, current conditions, and predictive analytics, AI enables businesses to make better-informed decisions. In finance, for instance, AI models can predict stock trends or assess the risk of loan applications with high accuracy. Similarly, in retail, AI tools analyze consumer behavior and preferences, helping companies make data-driven decisions about product offerings, marketing strategies, and pricing models.

Customer Experience: AI is revolutionizing customer service and user experiences across industries. Personalization is a key area where AI excels—by understanding individual preferences and behaviors, businesses can tailor products, services, and marketing campaigns to meet each customer's needs. For instance, streaming platforms like Netflix and Spotify use AI to recommend content based on users' past viewing or listening habits. In retail, AI-driven recommendation engines suggest products to shoppers in real-time, enhancing the online shopping experience and driving sales. Additionally, virtual assistants powered by AI, like Apple's Siri or Amazon's Alexa, provide instant responses to customer queries, ensuring a seamless and efficient user experience.

As these AI capabilities continue to evolve, the potential to further enhance efficiency, refine decision-making, and create more engaging customer experiences grows exponentially. In the following sections, we'll explore how these innovations are being realized in specific industries, with a particular focus on the groundbreaking partnership between Salesforce and NVIDIA, and how it is shaping the future of AI-powered business solutions.

Chapter 5: The Human-AI Collaboration

As AI continues to advance, the relationship between humans and machines is rapidly evolving. Far from replacing workers, AI technologies like those being developed by Salesforce and NVIDIA are designed to augment human capabilities and create more efficient, innovative work environments.

In the past, the introduction of new technologies in the workplace often led to concerns about job displacement. However, the latest generation of AI is more about collaboration than replacement. **Autonomous AI agents** are being built to work alongside humans, handling routine tasks and providing data-driven insights that allow employees to focus on more creative, strategic aspects of their roles.

For instance, in customer service, AI-powered chatbots can manage initial inquiries, resolving simple issues or directing customers to the right department. Meanwhile, human agents can devote more time to complex cases that require emotional intelligence, problem-solving, and empathy. This kind of collaboration allows businesses to operate at higher speeds and with greater accuracy, while also improving employee satisfaction by reducing mundane tasks.

Additionally, AI tools are empowering workers to make more informed decisions faster. By analyzing vast amounts of data in real time, AI systems can provide actionable insights that might take humans hours or even days to uncover. This ability to process and analyze data quickly and efficiently can lead to more timely, strategic decisions across all levels of an organization.

Moreover, the **human-AI collaboration** model is helping businesses create more personalized and impactful customer experiences. For example, AI systems can analyze customer preferences and behavior to offer tailored recommendations or support, enhancing customer satisfaction and loyalty. This dynamic interaction between AI and human workers is gradually reshaping industries across the board.

While AI is undeniably transforming the workplace, it's crucial to acknowledge the challenges that come with this shift. The successful integration of AI requires thoughtful consideration of ethical issues, training programs to equip workers with new skills, and a cultural shift towards embracing technology as a partner rather than a threat. As this relationship continues to evolve, it will define the future of work for generations to come.

The evolving relationship between AI and humans in the workplace is not just about replacing jobs but about **collaboration**. In many industries, AI tools are being used to augment human abilities, allowing workers to focus on more strategic tasks while AI handles repetitive or data-intensive processes. This shift toward collaboration models is visible across sectors like healthcare, finance, and retail.

For instance, in healthcare, **AI-powered diagnostic tools** help doctors analyze medical images faster and more accurately, allowing them to spend more time with patients rather than on manual analysis. In finance, AI chatbots handle customer service queries, while human agents are freed up to handle more complex financial advising tasks.

In **retail**, companies like Amazon use AI for inventory management and personalized customer recommendations, empowering human employees to improve in-store experiences and customer service. These examples highlight a growing trend: AI is a tool that enhances human capabilities, rather than replacing them entirely.

As AI continues to integrate into the workplace, questions around **ethics** and **human oversight** become increasingly important. AI systems, especially those that make decisions or interact with customers, must be designed with fairness, transparency, and accountability in mind. This ensures that the decisions made by AI are ethical and aligned with human values.

For example, in hiring practices, AI can be used to screen resumes or assess job candidates, but it must be carefully monitored to ensure that it doesn't reinforce existing biases. Human oversight is necessary to intervene in situations where AI may inadvertently favor one group over another, ensuring that the system operates in a fair and unbiased manner.

Furthermore, there is a growing conversation around the need for **AI regulation**. Governments and organizations are working together to set standards and regulations for AI to ensure it is developed and deployed responsibly. This includes protecting data privacy, ensuring algorithmic transparency, and holding companies accountable for the outcomes of AI systems.

AI's role in the workplace, when used correctly, can create an environment where technology and humans work hand-in-hand to improve productivity, innovation, and job satisfaction. However, the importance of **ethical oversight** cannot be overstated, as AI has the potential to greatly impact both individuals and society.

Chapter 6: The Future of AI: What's Next?

The future of AI and autonomous agents is nothing short of revolutionary. Experts across industries predict that we are on the cusp of a paradigm shift that will dramatically alter the way businesses operate, how work is performed, and even the relationship between humans and machines.

In the coming years, autonomous AI agents will likely become an integral part of everyday business operations, handling everything from routine customer service tasks to complex data analysis and decision-making. These agents are expected to grow more sophisticated, learning and adapting in real-time to new situations, much like humans do. This evolution will enable businesses to operate with unprecedented speed and accuracy.

Key predictions for the future include:

1. **Widespread Adoption Across Sectors**: As AI agents become more capable, industries like healthcare, finance, and retail will see a surge in

automation. For example, in healthcare, AI agents could assist with diagnosing medical conditions, analyzing patient data, and even providing personalized treatment recommendations. In finance, AI could revolutionize risk assessment, investment strategies, and fraud detection.

2. **Increased Collaboration Between Humans and AI**: Rather than replacing humans, AI is expected to augment human capabilities. Collaborative models where AI agents and human workers work together will become more common. This could lead to higher productivity, more informed decision-making, and improved innovation, as AI frees up human employees to focus on higher-level tasks.

3. **Smarter, More Autonomous Systems**: The ability of AI systems to operate autonomously will only improve. These agents will learn from vast amounts of data and improve their performance over time, reducing the need for

human intervention. The development of "self-learning" AI agents will allow businesses to automate tasks that previously required human judgment.

4. **AI as a Strategic Business Tool**: Companies will begin to leverage AI agents not just for operational efficiency, but as strategic tools. AI will be used to analyze market trends, predict consumer behavior, and identify new business opportunities, providing companies with a competitive edge in an increasingly data-driven world.

5. **Ethical Considerations and Human Oversight**: With the growing reliance on autonomous AI agents, ethical considerations will take center stage. How decisions made by AI systems impact individuals and society will be a critical concern. This will likely lead to the establishment of new regulatory frameworks and ethical guidelines for AI deployment. Human oversight will remain essential to ensure

that AI systems operate in a fair, transparent, and responsible manner.

In summary, the future of AI and autonomous agents is a landscape of rapid growth and transformative change. While challenges remain—particularly in terms of ethics and regulation—the potential benefits for businesses, workers, and society as a whole are immense. As AI continues to evolve, its role in the workplace and beyond will be a defining feature of the next generation of technology.

As powerful as AI is, its rapid evolution raises important ethical questions and concerns. One of the major risks is the displacement of workers. Automation could replace many jobs, particularly those that involve repetitive tasks. While AI will create new roles and industries, the transition could leave a significant portion of the workforce unprepared for these shifts.

Another major concern is data privacy and security. AI systems depend on massive amounts of data to function effectively, raising questions about who owns this data and how it's used. The potential for misuse—whether by corporations, governments, or malicious actors—poses a significant risk to individual freedoms and privacy.

Moreover, there are deep ethical dilemmas around decision-making by AI. How can we ensure that AI systems make fair, unbiased decisions? Who is accountable if an AI makes a harmful mistake? As these systems take on more responsibilities, it will be critical to establish clear ethical guidelines and robust human oversight mechanisms to mitigate these risks.

Conclusion

The AI revolution is not just on the horizon—it is here, reshaping how businesses operate and interact with customers, how industries innovate, and how individuals work. From autonomous AI agents to sophisticated decision-making systems, AI is revolutionizing everything from healthcare to finance, retail to manufacturing. As we've explored in this book, the technological advancements in AI, driven by partnerships like that of Salesforce and NVIDIA, are opening doors to efficiencies, insights, and opportunities previously unimaginable.

At the heart of this transformation lies the powerful partnership between Salesforce and NVIDIA. Their collaboration is not just a response to the evolving needs of the AI landscape; it is a proactive leap into the future of intelligent business solutions. Salesforce brings its vast ecosystem of CRM and business tools, while NVIDIA offers the processing power and AI innovation needed to fuel the next generation of autonomous agents. Together, they are laying the groundwork for a new era of AI-driven business operations, one where machines work hand-in-hand with humans to create more personalized, efficient, and impactful experiences.

Looking forward, businesses must embrace the inevitability of AI. Early adoption of AI technologies can provide a competitive edge, but only those who actively collaborate, experiment, and integrate these advancements will truly thrive. For companies like Salesforce and NVIDIA, the future is not just about automating tasks, but creating smarter solutions that can anticipate and meet the dynamic needs of their customers.

The path forward requires careful planning, strategic investment, and, above all, ethical consideration. As businesses adopt AI technologies, they must ensure that these tools are used responsibly—accountable to both their human workforce and the customers they serve. AI is poised to reshape our world, but it is the human element, the thoughtful oversight and collaboration, that will ensure these technologies deliver their full potential.

www.ingramcontent.com/pod-product-compliance
Lightning Source LLC
Chambersburg PA
CBHW070959240526
45469CB00017B/2485